DATE DUE

Ideas of the Modern World

Protesting Capitalism

R. G. Grant

Chicago, Illinois

© 2004 Raintree
Published by Raintree, a division of Reed Elsevier, Inc.
Chicago, Illinois
Customer Service 888-363-4266
Visit our website at www.raintreelibrary.com

All rights reserved. No part of this book may be reproduced or utilized in any form or by any means, electronic or mechanical, including photocopying, recording, or by any information storage and retrieval system, without permission in writing from the publishers. Inquiries should be addressed to:

Copyright Permissions
Raintree
100 N. LaSalle
Suite 1200
Chicago, IL 60602

Library of Congress Cataloging-in-Publication Data:
Grant, R. G.
  Protesting capitalism / R.G. Grant.
    v. cm. -- (Ideas of the modern world)
  Includes bibliographical references and index.
  Contents: Protest on the streets -- The rise of capitalism -- The
  alternative vision -- Communism and social democracy -- The third world
  and the new left -- Opposing global capitalism -- Into the twenty-first
  century -- Glossary.
    ISBN 0-7398-6414-9 (Library Binding-hardcover)
    1. Capitalism--Juvenile literature. 2. Capitalism--History--Juvenile
  literature. 3. Protest movements--Juvenile literature. [1. Capitalism.
  2. Protest movements.] I. Title. II. Series.
   HB501.G6295 2004
    330.12'2--dc21

2003002066

1 2 3 4 5 6 7 8 9 0
LB 08 07 06 05 04

Acknowledgments
The author and publishers thank the following for permission to reproduce photographs:

Title and contents page, pp. 4, 7, 35, 51, 52, 56, 57 Popperfoto/Reuters; pp. 6, 15, 39, 41, 42, 47, 48 Rex Features; pp. 8, 9, 18, 32, 33,45 AKG London; p. 10 Mary Evans/Tom Morgan; pp. 13, 16, 21, 22, 23 Mary Evans Picture Library; p. 20 AKG Photo; pp. 25, 28, 29 (left) 36, 43, 59 Popperfoto p. 27 Hodder Wayland Picture Library/UPI; p .29, 34 Corbis: 29(right) Ecoscene/Corbis, 34 (Wayne Lawler); p. 37 Hodder Wayland Picture Library/Cubafotos/John Griffiths; p. 31 Hodder Wayland Picture Library/Gordon Clements.

Cover photo shows protesters blocking a police line from moving forward during the World Trade Organization summit in Seattle on November 30, 1999 (Popperfoto).

Printed in Hong Kong

Contents

Protest on the Streets					4

The Rise of Capitalism				8

The Alternative Vision				15

Communism and Social Democracy			24

Developing Nations and the New Left		34

Opposing Global Capitalism			46

Into the 21st Century				56

Timeline					60

Further Reading				61

Glossary					62

Index						64

Protest on the Streets

In November and December 1999, more than 50,000 protesters gathered on the streets of Seattle, Washington. Representatives of 135 countries, including then U.S. President Bill Clinton, were there to attend a summit meeting of the World Trade Organization (WTO). The summit was intended to continue the process known as **globalization**—the means by which different economies around the world become increasingly integrated into one large economy. With globalization trade and money flow freely from country to country. Businesses have access to a "global market"—selling and producing their product wherever they can or wherever labor is cheapest. The global market means that businesses can have access to cheaper imports and larger export markets. But these benefits are not necessarily shared by all and, although the protestors at the WTO summit were drawn from many different groups, they all agreed that unrestricted global **capitalism** was to be resisted.

Demonstrators block a street during the WTO summit in Seattle on November 30, 1999. The protests severely disrupted the summit meeting.

Making the rich richer

These antiglobalization protesters believed that globalization was being promoted by the governments of richer countries to allow big business to **exploit** the earth's people and natural resources. They believed this was a policy that was making the rich richer and the poor poorer. At the same time they felt it was destroying the environment and undermining established cultures and ways of life. The protesters felt they were standing up for ordinary people who were powerless in the face of decisions made by the world's political and business leaders —decisions that could have a devastating effect on the lives of individuals.

Direct attacks

A small minority of the demonstrators in Seattle were bent on carrying out direct attacks on the objects of their anger. They smashed the windows of branches of multinational businesses such as Starbucks, McDonalds, and Gap. As the police confronted the protesters, firing plastic bullets and tear gas, the center of Seattle was reduced to a battleground. For a time the WTO summit was paralyzed, with senior politicians and their officials trapped in their hotels. Whereas nonviolent protest might have been ignored, the violent chaos captured headlines across the world.

Seattle in 1999 was only one example of the antiglobalization demonstrations that now accompany most summit meetings of world leaders or finance ministers. Now wherever such meetings take place, heavily armed police are there in force. In the summer of 2001, during a meeting of world leaders in Genoa, Italy, a demonstrator was killed during violent clashes between protesters and police. Although only tiny numbers took part in the violence that attracted so much publicity, there was no doubt that millions of people worldwide sympathized with the protesters' resistance to the way the world's economy was being run.

Rich against poor

One radical group, the League of Revolutionaries for a New America, declared after the 1999 protests in Seattle:

"The huge protests against the World Trade Organization's meeting in Seattle were a reflection of a confrontation which is gathering momentum—the confrontation between the world's rich and the world's poor."

Riot police fire tear gas to disperse demonstrators during the meeting of world leaders in Genoa, Italy, July 2001.

Anticapitalism

These protest movements have often been referred to as "anticapitalist" (opposing capitalism). **Capitalism** is an **economic system** in which the tools or machines used to create products are privately owned. It is based on the idea that freedom and prosperity are maximized when individuals and businesses make as much money as possible by selling goods and services. To do this they constantly search out new ways of producing things more cheaply. One way to do this is to find ways to minimize labor costs.

Capitalism is also known as a **free-market** economy or free enterprise. Because of the word "free," free market and free enterprise both imply that people have the right to own property, and to do what they wish

Mixed and merry

Anticapitalism protesters are a diverse group and they often create a carnival-like atmosphere. Richard Swift, co-editor of the radical magazine *New Internationalist*, described an anticapitalist protest in Quebec, Canada in 2001:

"Imagination was not in short supply. A contingent [group] dressed in black-and-white uniforms marched as 'Mad Cows Against Globalization.' A huge Ronald McDonald swayed over the crowd with large bags of money in either hand.... There were Haitian contingents, local Mobilization for Global Justice coalitions (MOBforGLOB) from New Jersey to Ottawa, people from all over Latin America, the World March of Women, and LOLA (Little Old Lady Activists)."

Protest on the Streets

> ## Capitalism good for the poor
>
> Writing in the solidly procapitalist newspaper *The Times* in March 2002, journalist Rosemary Righter criticized the thinking of those who demonstrated against capitalism:
>
> *"These are highly diverse groups ... but what they have in common is detestation of ... capitalism, multinational corporations, free capital markets.... The poor they say must be 'protected' from these forces—protected, that is, from the things that have made their own societies rich."*

with their property. In economics property refers not only to something like a book or a television, but also to the **means of production,** that is, the way the book or television is produced, and to the labor that goes into making the product. In a free-market economy one can buy or sell his or her property (or labor or product) for whatever price he or she wants. Presumably, this means that competition between different producers or owners ensures that prices are always as low as they can possibly be.

Global capitalism means breaking down trade barriers so that the whole world is an open market. This means that if you had a product to sell, you could try to sell it to your next-door neighbor or to someone who lives in a different country. People in protest movements believe that more restrictions or controls are needed on the activities of the multinational businesses (businesses with branches in several countries) that dominate the world economy, and on big investors shifting millions of dollars around the globe.

The desire to resist, reform, or overthrow global capitalism is not just a recent development; it has a long and colorful history.

An anticapitalist protester wearing a jester's hat and a gas mask demonstrates near the site of the Summit of the Americas in Quebec City, Canada, April 22, 2001.

7

The Rise of Capitalism

The rise of modern global **capitalism** can be traced back to the start of the Industrial Revolution in Western countries. This change was first evident in Britain. Beginning in 1780 enterprising British businessmen began to invest in new machinery powered by steam or water. The use of these machines, operated by workers in large-scale factories, allowed Britain's production of cotton goods to multiply 50 times between 1785 and 1850.

The output of other industries, such as pottery-making and iron-founding, also grew steeply, as did production from coal mines. This Industrial Revolution was linked to changing attitudes toward business. The idea spread that allowing businessmen to pursue profit and trade without restrictions or interference from government (that is, in a **free market**) was the best way to increase national wealth. The combination of business enterprise with the use of machines in factories is sometimes called "industrial capitalism."

★ Luddites

In 1811 skilled workers in the English counties of Nottinghamshire, Lancashire, and Yorkshire began destroying newly introduced textile machinery. Known as "Luddites," after their leader, Ned Ludd, they rightly feared that the machines would destroy their livelihood by making goods faster and cheaper than they could on their hand looms. The movement continued for several years but was eventually supressed by the authorities. Many Luddites were hanged or deported to Australia. "Luddite" has since become a term used for anyone who opposes the introduction of new technology.

In the 1800s new machinery rapidly increased output of manufactured goods, making fortunes for factory owners. This is the first steam hammer, invented in 1842.

Economic growth

Industrialization at first affected only a small minority of the population, even in Britain. But during the course of the 1800s, industrial capitalism generated massive economic growth. The money made from producing goods more quickly and cheaply was invested in building more factories and mines and constructing more new machinery. There seemed to be no limit to the expanding production and technological innovation, or to the money being made from both. Parts of Europe and the United States followed in Britain's wake, chasing and in many cases overtaking the British in industrial output. By 1914 people were producing 50 times more goods and services worldwide than they had in the 1780s. Most of this extra production was in Western Europe and North America.

Unhealthy conditions

Despite its ability to generate such vast wealth, the rise of industrial capitalism initially had a grim effect on the lives of working people. Many craftsmen lost their livelihood as new machinery replaced their skills with simple repetitive tasks, often carried out by unskilled women and children who were cheaper to employ. Conditions in factories and mines were usually terrible. Workers were made to work excessively long hours for low wages in an environment that was unhealthy and often downright dangerous. There was nothing new about poverty or hard work. But in the first half of the 19th century, the sight of the filthy, unsanitary new industrial towns, such as Manchester in northern England, shocked everyone who visited them.

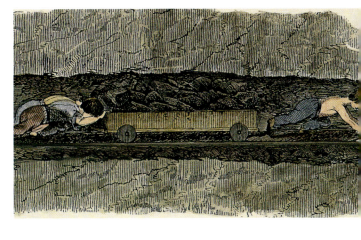

During the Industrial Revolution, working people labored for long hours in bad conditions for low pay. Here children haul coal in a mine shaft in the 1840s.

Protesting Capitalism

At the same time, traditional forms of support and protection for working people and the poor were swept aside as being against the spirit of **capitalism.** Enterprising people were encouraged to make their fortunes, but the less fortunate were left to fend for themselves. Traditional forms of charity for the poor in time of need were denounced by the supporters of capitalism as undermining the will to work. Previously many skilled workers had belonged to guilds, organizations that protected their interests and guaranteed them employment, while also fixing wages and prices. Now guilds were abolished. Workers were "free" to sell their labor to whoever would employ them for whatever wage they could get. They could also be laid off by employers whenever they were no longer needed.

Child labor

In the 1800s many European countries passed laws limiting or banning the use of child labor in factories and mines. However, in the United States business owners remained free to **exploit** children as cheap workers. Around 1900 it was common, for example, for the children of newly arrived immigrants in New York to work for up to sixteen hours a day in dangerous, disease-ridden factories. These factories were known as "sweatshops" because the work there was so hard.

Workers' revolt

With their livelihoods threatened, some workers resisted in the most direct way, by machine-breaking.

Direct action: Luddites smash textile machinery.

Tolpuddle Martyrs

In the 1800s, many workers who reacted to exploitation by forming labor unions faced harsh persecution. In 1834 six farm laborers from the village of Tolpuddle in Dorset, southwest England, were exiled as criminals to Australia for forming a union to resist a cut in their wages. Their harsh sentence provoked a national outcry, and they were freed two years later. On his return one of the "martyrs," George Loveless, called on workers to join together to defend their rights: "Let every working man come forward," he wrote, "from east to west, and from north to south, unite firmly but peaceably together as the heart of one man."

This happened both in towns and in the countryside—for example, British farm workers wrecked agricultural machinery in the 1830s. Some workers tried to form **labor unions** to defend their interests, fighting for higher wages and recognition of craft skills. But unions remained illegal, and faced brutal repression by the authorities.

Reform

Over time criticism of the poor working conditions that industrial capitalism produced, and fear of a workers' revolt, led to a steady trickle of reforms. In many European countries, governments intervened to ban child labor and limit working hours in factories and mines.

By 1914 the introduction of state pensions and unemployment insurance had begun to soften the harshness of working-class life, especially in Germany and Britain. Factory workers also began to share modestly in rising wealth, and became consumers of the new cheap goods that industry produced. Much of the ordinary working population of Western Europe and North America was, by 1914, far better off than a century before—although great inequality between rich and poor remained.

Effect on the rest of the world

From the beginning the impact of industrial capitalism was felt on a worldwide scale. The booming British textile industry imported raw cotton from abroad—causing, for instance, a huge expansion in slave-worked cotton plantations in the southern United States. A large proportion of the products of the British cotton mills were sold abroad. India, once a place that produced textiles for export to Europe, had by 1850 become a large-scale importer of cotton goods made in Lancashire.

Countries could not choose to stay outside the new global economy dominated by the industrializing West. The Industrial Revolution gave the Western powers weapons far superior to any elsewhere in the world, from machine-guns to iron steam-powered gunboats. The so-called Opium Wars (1839–1842 and 1856–1860) made the proud Chinese Empire open its doors to foreign trade. Japan, where the *shoguns* (local rulers) exercised tight control on trade with the outside world, was threatened by a fleet of U.S. warships commanded by Commodore Perry in 1853–1854 and was forced to begin opening its

★ The Opium Wars

In the early 1800s, British merchants were determined to open up trade with China. They had two problems: The Chinese authorities wanted to keep foreign trade under strict control, and the Chinese did not want any of the goods the British had to sell. The British eventually found a product that the Chinese consumers would buy—the drug opium, produced from poppies in British-ruled India. Understandably the Chinese authorities did not want their people to become drug addicts, and tried to stop the opium trade. In 1839 the British responded by waging war on China. Defeated, the Chinese were forced to open ports to British trade. A further war in 1856, in which Britain was aided by France, forced China to abandon all attempts to exclude foreign goods or investment. China became an open field for European and North American capitalists to **exploit** at will.

ports. In many places Europeans seized direct control of territory that became a part of worldwide empires. Most of Africa, India, and southeast Asia was under European rule by 1900.

Following the West

Given the overwhelming economic and military success of Western Europe and North America, those countries that could tried to imitate them, developing their own industries and adopting

During the first Opium War, Britain's Royal Navy destroyed the warships of the Chinese Empire with superior guns produced by the factories of the Industrial Revolution.

Westernized styles of government and society. Japan was the most successful at this, and from 1868 onward created its own industrial revolution. But the West did not favor industrial development in Asia, South America, or Africa. Western investment created new ports, roads, and railroads in these regions to **exploit** previously untouched mineral resources and develop agricultural production. But this was so that these regions could supply cheap raw materials to, and buy manufactured products from, factories in Europe and North America. The West did not intend that these countries should compete with it.

By 1914 global **capitalism** was generating huge profits for investors, businessmen, and financiers in Europe and North America. It was also generating enough wealth to give benefits and new opportunities to ordinary working people in these industrial heartlands. But at the same time, it faced **socialism,** a large-scale movement that took an alternative view of the future, and hoped and expected to replace capitalist civilization with something more just and more efficient.

★ Conservative anticapitalists

Much of the early opposition to the rise of the new industrial capitalists and their way of doing business came from conservatives—people who wanted society to stay the same or turn backwards. This feeling was especially strong among rural landowners, who had traditionally enjoyed a dominant position in society. Conservatives argued that life had been better for working people when they had been tied to the land, serving a local lord or squire all their lives. This was preferable, they claimed, to being capitalist "free labor," which meant taking whatever job they could find, or enduring spells of unemployment. Even slave owners in the southern United States used this argument, claiming their slaves were more secure and better cared-for than "free" factory workers in the northern United States. Very few slaves seem to have agreed with their owners on this point.

The Alternative Vision

Socialism first appeared in the early 1800s. This was a time when the idea of political equality—that all people should have the same rights, such as the right to vote—was winning increasing acceptance. Socialists extended the idea of equality to social and economic life. They argued that political equality was meaningless if most people were living in poverty in a society dominated by a minority of the rich.

Throughout the 1800s, the right to vote was extended to people in many countries. Here voting takes place in Cheyenne, Wyoming, the first state to give women the vote.

A better world?

Early socialists (often called utopian socialists) put forward idealistic projects to create a kinder, better world. They imagined a society based on harmony and cooperation, rather than on competition and greed. **Capitalism** saw society as made up of individuals pursuing their personal advantage and satisfaction. But, socialists argued, the success of enterprising capitalists was often at other people's expense. If society were run differently, they said, people could live peacefully in communities where wealth was shared equally, where necessary work was performed cheerfully and without compulsion. This would be an **egalitarian** society—one in which no one had more money or property than anyone else.

Visions of Utopia

In 1891 Irish author Oscar Wilde, a supporter of **socialism** in the late 1800s, argued that humanity needed visions of an ideal society, or "Utopia," to aim at, even if they might seem unrealistic:

"A map of the world that does not include Utopia is not worth even glancing at, for it leaves out the one country at which Humanity is always landing. And when Humanity lands there, it looks out, and, seeing a better country, sets sail. Progress is the realization of Utopias."

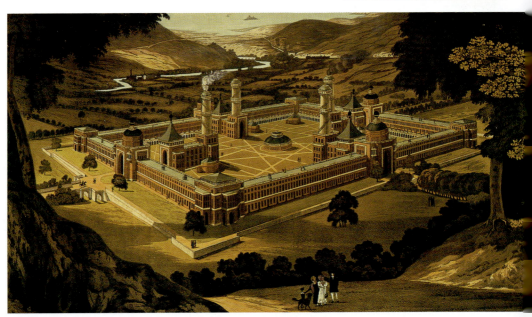

British socialist Robert Owen founded his industrial community at New Harmony, Indiana in 1825. Owen hoped it would be a model for a future society based on equality and cooperation.

Self-governing communities

Two early leading socialists were Robert Owen in Britain and Charles Fourier in France. Owen, who rose from being an assistant in the textile trade to become a wealthy cotton-mill owner, created an industrial community at New Lanark in Scotland that he hoped would point the way to a better society. About 2,000 workers were housed in clean, identical living quarters with facilities that included a concert hall and a lecture theater. Owen went on to establish a self-governing egalitarian community in New Harmony, Indiana in 1825.

This bold experiment in communal living was not a permanent success. Nor were similar **communes** set up by Fourier's followers in the 1830s, also in the United States (chosen because there was plenty of land and the authorities were less likely to interfere). In truth these early socialists were often far from realistic. Fourier, for example, argued that all the most dirty and disgusting jobs in society could be done by small children, since children have a natural love of dirt. Above all they had little idea of how to move from the existing society to a future egalitarian socialist society. Their plans simply required people to have a sudden change of heart.

Cooperative movements

Many working people and small producers in the 1800s were drawn to setting up "cooperatives." These businesses were run cooperatively for the equal benefit of all involved not, as in the capitalist economy, for the competitive, profit-making interests of a handful of owners. In Britain, for example, 28 Lancashire working men opened a cooperative shop in Toad Lane, Rochdale, in 1844. From these humble beginnings, British cooperative stores grew into a nationwide movement. Regular "co-op" shoppers became, in effect, **shareholders** in their stores. In other countries producers' cooperatives were more important, with large numbers of small farmers joining together to market their produce. In Denmark, for example, by 1892 there were more than 1,000 cooperative dairies. Most Danish bacon, eggs, milk, and fruit was produced and marketed cooperatively. Both cooperative stores and producers' cooperatives have continued to flourish up to the present day in many parts of the world, including the United States.

Karl Marx, left, and Friedrich Engels were lifelong collaborators in the struggle to overthrow capitalism.

Class conflict

Socialism only became a major force when its ideas began to relate to social and political conflict in the 1800s. The person largely responsible for making this link was the German thinker and **political activist** Karl Marx. For Marx the key to understanding what was happening in the world lay in what he called **class conflict**. If a socialist society was going to come about, he argued, it would be through a revolt of the mass of factory workers—the working class or the **proletariat**.

At the time, according to Marx, society was ruled by the **bourgeoisie**—industrialists, financiers, and property owners—who robbed the workers by paying them much less for their work than the things they produced were worth. But, said Marx, the workers would one day rise up against bourgeois rule and take power for themselves. This revolution or class conflict would result in a workers'

Workers unite!

From early on the struggle for socialism was seen as a global struggle, one that workers should join regardless of nationality. Karl Marx's *Communist Manifesto* of 1848 concluded with a famous call to action:

"The workers have nothing to lose but their chains. They have a world to win. Workers of the world, unite!"

government that would take factories and businesses away from their owners and run them for the benefit of the workers, ending the system of labor for private profit. This would lead eventually to communism, a state of perfect equality, freedom, and self-fulfilment for all.

The overthrow of capitalism

Marx's vision, developed in his writings over many years, became very influential. His work established the idea that **capitalism** was the cause of the world's woes and that the overthrow of capitalism was the way forward for humanity. Marx did not, however, want to turn the clock back to before the industrial age. He believed that industrialization made a future equal society possible, as enough goods could be produced for everyone, and no one need be poor. His vision seemed to show that the overthrow of capitalism was not just desirable, but inevitable—the necessary next stage in the evolution of human society.

Marx's view of the industrial working class as the people who would start a socialist revolution made sense, since they were growing in numbers and, in many cases, were angry about the conditions in which they lived and worked. Workers were naturally drawn to coming together to try to improve their lives, since individually they had no power and few opportunities.

Karl Marx

Born in Trier, Germany, Karl Marx (1818–1883) spent most of his life in London because, as a political activist, he could have been arrested in mainland Europe. With his lifelong associate Friedrich Engels, he wrote and organized tirelessly to undermine the capitalist system. His *Communist Manifesto*, a rousing call for a worldwide workers' revolution, appeared in 1848, and the first volume of his massive analysis of the capitalist system, *Das Kapital* (Capital), followed in 1867. Marx was more successful as a writer than in practical politics. The First International Working Men's Association, which he helped to set up in 1864 to organize socialists from different countries into a single movement, fell apart amid bitter divisions in 1872. Although Marx was unwavering in his absolute opposition to capitalism, his ideas varied over time. After his death some of his thoughts were shaped into a rigid way of thinking, Marxism. It has been correctly said that Marx was not himself a **Marxist**.

Protesting Capitalism

Workers' struggle
Labor unions became features of industrial society. Unions allowed workers to gather in a collective struggle for better pay and conditions. The socialist argument that employers were idle parasites living off the sweat of the workers corresponded to most working people's view of their own situation.

The capitalist system, however, proved far tougher than its enemies first believed. When Marx published his *Communist Manifesto* in 1848, he was convinced that **capitalism** was on its last legs. But a spate of revolutionary uprisings across Europe in that year—in which socialists of various kinds played a limited but significant part—were put down without achieving any fundamental social change. Further popular uprisings in Paris in 1871, in Russia in 1905, and in Barcelona in 1909 were also defeated.

Socialist programs
Although the expected revolution to replace capitalism by a new kind of society did not come, socialist movements grew to be a major influence in Europe (much less so in the United States). In countries such as Britain, France, and Germany, political parties with socialist programs—ranging

Protesters on the march during the revolutionary uprising in Russia in 1905. Their banners include one repeating Marx's slogan: "Workers of the world, unite!"

from "minimum" demands such as for a legal limit on working time to eight hours a day to "maximum" aims for the eventual takeover of all large businesses by the state—won the majority of working-class votes.

Such parties, like the labor unions to which they were linked, attributed many of the world's ills, especially the existence of poverty and inequality, on financiers and industrialists. But in day-to-day political life, they concentrated on promoting gradual reforms, for example, winning reductions in working hours. This reflected the basic concerns of most of their working-class supporters. Inevitably there were groups of revolutionary **extremists**, notably **anarchists**, who opposed this gradual reform and called for absolute opposition to capitalism and the ruling classes.

A demonstration by labor unionists in Manchester in 1874: The unions expressed the workers' sense of solidarity in opposition to their employers.

Anarchism

Anarchism is a movement that developed in the 1800s, mostly through the influence of French thinker Pierre Joseph Proudhon (1809–1865) and Russian activist Mikhail Bakunin (1814–1876). Hostile to **hierarchical** government of any kind, anarchists believed that small-scale self-governing communities would be the building blocks of a new society. They rejected taking part in parliamentary elections or in negotiations to improve workers' conditions. Instead many of them recommended "direct action" against governments and capitalists. This sometimes meant the assassination of political leaders and **militant** strike action by anarchist trade unionists, known as "**anarcho-syndicalists**." Although their ideal was a world of perfect peace and harmony, many anarchists believed violence was essential to shake the foundations of the capitalist order. Bakunin declared that "the passion for destruction is at the same time a creative passion."

Violent gestures

Through the late 1800s and early 1900s, there were many attacks, including assassinations of political leaders carried out by anarchists. One of the victims was U.S. President William McKinley, shot dead by **anarchist** Leon Czolgosz in 1901. Some anarchists described such actions as "**propaganda** by the deed," violent gestures that would draw attention to the injustice and oppression in the world.

Although condemning such extremism, more mainstream socialists did not accept that their role was simply to improve the workers' lot within capitalist society. The German Social Democrat Party adopted Marxism as its **ideology**, while the British Labour (the British spelling of labor) Party did not. But both at least in theory looked forward to the day when the capitalist system would be replaced with a socialist alternative. Socialist parties were reluctant to consider compromising their principles by taking part in running a capitalist state, although the Social Democrats in Denmark broke ranks to take a share in government starting in 1913.

The anarchist Leon Czolgosz assassinates the president of the United States, William McKinley, on September 6, 1901.

★ Industrial Workers of the World

Probably the most impressive anticapitalism organization ever created in the United States was the Industrial Workers of the World (IWW), founded in Chicago in 1905. This was an **anarcho-syndicalist** movement dedicated to using **labor union** action to confront and ultimately overthrow capitalist society. The IWW organized a series of major strikes during which workers engaged in direct action against employers—one of its slogans was "negotiate with dynamite." It hoped one day for a "general strike" of all workers to bring about the downfall of **capitalism.** The IWW grew to have about 100,000 members. When the United States entered World War I in 1917, however, the IWW, which opposed the war, was weakened by the authorities. Its organization was broken up and many of its activists jailed.

Emma Goldman

Emma Goldman was one of the most prominent American anarchists of her day. Born in Lithuania in 1869, she emigrated to the United States when she was 16. There she met her lifelong companion, Alexander Berkman, and became involved in anarchist politics. In 1892 Goldman and Berkman planned revenge on Pennsylvania steel company chairman Henry Clay Frick, who had used armed police to shoot striking workers. Berkman shot and stabbed Frick, but failed to kill him, and was imprisoned for 14 years. An inspired public speaker, Goldman continued to advocate anarchist principles and oppose the rich and powerful. After assassinating President McKinley in 1901, anarchist Leon Czolgosz described himself as "a disciple of Emma Goldman—her words set me on fire." Goldman herself was repeatedly imprisoned and eventually, in 1919, deported from the United States to Russia and deprived of her citizenship. She hated the communist regime in Russia and later renounced her belief in acts of violence. But up to her death in 1940 she never lost her faith in the possibility of creating a freer world by the overthrow of existing capitalist society. She was also a leading activist for women's rights.

May Day

By 1914, in the European heartlands of industrial capitalism, **mass movements** existed that were dedicated, at least in theory, to overthrowing the capitalist system. In 1890, May Day was established as an annual socialist festival. Every year on this day millions of workers in different countries marched under red banners, the symbol of **socialism.** In 1889 the Second International was set up. This was an organization that brought together socialist parties from different countries. They agued that that they had common interests and policies that went beyond national boundaries. Socialists confidently expected that one day the workers would inherit the Earth. But what actually happened next—World War I—was a shock to both the capitalist system and to its enemies.

Anarchist Emma Goldman

Communism and Social Democracy

During the 20th century, the only practical attempt to create and run an alternative to **capitalism** was made by the countries that adopted communism. Another emerging trend saw **social democrats** in charge of the governments of capitalist states running capitalist economies.

World War I (1914–1918) brought all the major industrial countries into conflict. The vast resources of industrial capitalism were devoted to the work of the war, which led to the deaths of about ten million people. The war was a disaster for the capitalist system, creating political and economic instability that would last for decades. But it was also, in its way, a disaster for international **socialism**.

Before 1914 socialists had claimed that workers across the world had more in common with one another

Vladimir Ilyich Lenin

When Lenin (1870–1924) was an adolescent, his elder brother was executed for his part in a plot to assassinate Tsar Alexander III. Lenin became a revolutionary activist, adopting Marxism and helping found a Russian Social Democrat party. In 1903 he caused a split in the Social Democrats that left him as leader of the hardline Bolshevik faction. Lenin was living in exile in Switzerland when the Tsarist government in Russia was overthrown in February 1917. He returned to Russia and led the Bolsheviks to seize power in November 1917. Lenin refused to allow other socialist groups any share in the new government. He believed that the only way to make a successful revolution was through the leadership of a disciplined revolutionary party. In practice this meant that his communist state became a single-party dictatorship, without **democracy** or respect for individual freedom.

than with governments or employers in their own countries. However, workers flocked (or were drafted) to fight for their country during World War I, and most socialists supported their homeland. Only a small minority of socialists called for workers to shun the "capitalist war." One of these was the exiled leader of the Russian Bolshevik Party, Vladimir Ilyich Lenin, who saw the conflict as an opportunity at last to overthrow the capitalist system.

The October Revolution

As the war dragged on, with mounting casualties, initial enthusiasm evaporated and social conflicts surfaced once more. In February 1917 the Tsarist regime in Russia collapsed in the face of popular discontent. Lenin returned from exile and, that October, led the Bolsheviks—soon renamed "communists" —to seize power and proclaim a workers' state. Lenin's hope and expectation was that revolutionary socialists in other countries, especially Germany, would also take power. But despite widespread upheavals at the end of the war, and some shortlived attempts to found workers' states— for example, in Hungary and the German state of Bavaria—Russia was the only place in which a revolutionary government survived. In the absence of revolution elsewhere in the world, the Russian communists adopted the policy of "building socialism in a single country."

In 1917 armed workers, soldiers, and sailors gave Lenin's Bolsheviks the firepower to seize control of Russia.

The survival of Lenin's communist regime was achieved through an utterly ruthless suppression of all opposition. The communists did not hesitate to shoot workers who protested at the regime's policies. In 1923 the Union of Soviet Socialist Republics (USSR or Soviet Union) was formally founded, ruling most of the old territory of the Russian empire. It was a state in which all power was in the hands of a single organization, the Communist Party.

Social democrats

The revolution in Russia split the international socialist movement in two. Communist parties aligned with the Soviet Union opposed socialist parties that believed in democracy and individual freedom (**social democrats**). The social democrats shifted away from the idea of an overthrow of the capitalist system. Instead they wanted state control of only certain key areas of the economy—typically central banks, transportation, and the largest industries—and measures to make the distribution of wealth in society fairer, for example, by heavier taxation of the rich. Social democratic parties began to form governments. The Labour Party, for example, held power in Britain for the first time in 1924—without in any way overturning the basic order of society.

Communists

The communist parties, on the other hand, were committed to the overthrow of **capitalism** and of liberal democracy—the form of government most associated with free-market capitalism, involving the election of governments and parliaments and respect for individual human rights. The communist parties formed part of an organization, the Third International, based in Moscow. In practice their policies were dictated by the Soviet Union and often designed to serve Soviet interests. Communist activists accepted this, because they saw the survival

During the Great Depression, unemployed workers were reduced to standing in line for handouts of free food. This restaraunt, known as the "Free Lunch" was run by Chicago gangster Al Capone.

of the Soviet Union as an essential first step toward what would eventually be a world revolution.

The idea of a worldwide collapse of capitalism was far more believable in the 1920s and 1930s than it had been before World War I. Global capitalism pre-1914 was an immensely well-organized, coordinated system, with a large measure of free trade and financial stability. The attempt to recreate this system in the 1920s failed and, by 1930, the world was plunged into the Great Depression (see box), with mass unemployment and a catastrophic drop in world trade. Indeed, in the 1930s the free movement of goods and money around the world effectively ceased.

The Great Depression

The Great Depression was a worldwide economic slump in the early 1930s. It was triggered in the United States by the great **stock market** crash of 1929. The Depression brought mass unemployment and poverty to much of the world. Critics of capitalism saw the Great Depression as a clear example of the weakness of the capitalist system. The stock market crash, they felt, showed the harmful effects of financial speculation, which made the fate of nations turn on what was, in effect, no more than a gambling casino.

German dictator Adolf Hitler attends a military review during the rapid rearmament of Germany in the 1930s.

The rise of fascism

The Depression created a widespread feeling—felt well beyond socialist or communist circles—that capitalism had failed and was declining. Liberal democracy was also apparently in decline. Some countries in Western Europe became **right-wing** dictatorships, notably Italy, ruled by Benito Mussolini's Fascist Party, and Germany, ruled by Adolf Hitler's Nazi Party. Mussolini and Hitler opposed communism and **socialism,** and communists were put in concentration camps in Nazi Germany. Both dictators were more interested in using money and labor to increase their country's global power than in creating a **free-market** economy.

The New Deal

Even in the United States, where the stock market crash of 1929 was followed by mass unemployment, President Franklin D. Roosevelt's New Deal, although not socialist, was far removed from the traditional American belief in free enterprise. Under the New Deal of 1933, the government strove to provide work for the unemployed, give social security to the poor, and support the activities of **labor unions**.

The Soviet model

With capitalism apparently in disarray, it is hardly surprising that many people in the capitalist West were fascinated by the attempt to build a "socialist alternative" in the Soviet Union. During the 1920s in the Soviet Union, there was a large measure of state control and planning, but there was also some small-scale free enterprise. The latter existed especially in the country, where peasants kept the land they had seized during the revolution. Starting in 1929, under the **dictatorial** rule of Josef Stalin, this situation changed. The Soviet Union embarked on rapid industrialization, in which the state laid down production targets for each industry and assigned investment, labor, and materials as it thought appropriate. Agriculture was "collectivized"—meaning that the land was taken from the peasants to create large state-owned farms.

Leon Trotsky

Trotsky (original name Lev Davidovich Bronstein) was second only to Lenin as leader of the Russian Revolution. After Lenin's death in 1924, however, Trotsky lost out the power struggle with Stalin and was expelled from the Soviet Union in 1929. Trotsky argued that Stalin had betrayed the cause of international socialism, instead putting socialism at the service of his own dictatorship. He called for a "permanent revolution" that would stop oppressive **bureaucrats** from taking over the revolution, as he argued had happened in the Soviet Union. In 1940 Trotsky was murdered in Mexico by one of Stalin's agents. Trotskyism attracted those who held a traditional **Marxist** belief in a revolution based on the industrial working class, but who disliked Soviet-style communism.

Official Soviet photos of the 1930s showed well-fed Ukrainian peasants enjoying life on new collective farms. In reality the peasants endured brutal repression and mass starvation.

In the 1930s, as industry in the capitalist world stagnated or declined, Soviet industry expanded quickly. But the human cost was terrible. Turning farms into **collectives** led to mass starvation, especially in the Ukraine. Millions of Ukranians died, and millions of other Soviet citizens became political prisoners and were used as slave labor. Stalin turned the communist state into a personal dictatorship. Many thousands of dedicated communist activists, including most of the leaders of the 1917 revolution, were "purged" (killed or imprisoned) as Stalin rid himself of any possible opposition.

Yet many people, even inside the Soviet Union, continued to believe that this was merely the necessary cost of building a better future. In the West, communist sympathizers refused to believe reports of the horrors of Soviet life that appeared in the **bourgeois** press. Instead they believed ludicrously optimistic accounts of Soviet life written by people who supported the communist cause.

Anticolonialism
The example of Soviet communism inspired many of those in the developing world who wanted to liberate their countries from Western domination. Communists argued that China and India, Africa, and the West Indies could only ever be truly independent of the West if they withdrew from the capitalist system. Otherwise, even if they had their own governments, they would still suffer from economic exploitation by Western business interests. In their

Gandhi and civil disobedience
The most prominent anticolonialist leader of the 1920s and 1930s was the Indian nationalist Mohandas "Mahatma" Gandhi (1869–1948). Gandhi's greatest innovation in his campaign to end British rule in India was the use of **civil disobedience** as a form of protest and resistance. Protesters practicing civil disobedience were prepared to obstruct the authorities and deliberately break laws with which they disagreed, but were strictly nonviolent, even if attacked or arrested. Gandhi's example of nonviolent resistance has been used by many other protest movements, including anticapitalism ones, up to the present day.

Communism and Social Democracy

view, anticolonialism and anticapitalism were inextricably linked, because all the **colonial powers** were capitalist. The leaders of anticolonial movements in the 1930s included the communist Ho Chi Minh in Vietnam (then part of French Indochina). Many noncommunist anticolonialists, such as Jawaharlal Nehru in India, were strongly influenced by socialist ideas.

The power and political standing of the Soviet Union were massively increased by its successes during World War II, when it played a leading role in defeating Nazi Germany. This victory allowed the Soviet Union to set up communist regimes in Poland, Hungary, Czechoslovakia, Romania,

Mao Zedong

Chinese communist leader Mao Zedong (1893–1976) drew support mainly from peasants in the countryside rather than industrial workers in the cities. He won power in 1949 after building a peasant army to fight a **guerrilla** war against China's nationalist rulers. This led Mao to state, "Political power grows out of the barrel of a gun." Like Lenin in Russia, Mao established a single-party dictatorship in China. In the 1960s he turned against the Soviet Union, denouncing Soviet leaders for deserting true socialism. In 1966 he encouraged the Cultural Revolution, an uprising by young **extremists** in China against teachers, civil servants, and many other authority figures. Mao was an attractive figure to many Western radicals in the 1960s, and some Western students called themselves "Maoists." But since his death, there have been many revelations of the brutality, oppression, and corruption of his regime.

Chinese revolutionary and dictator Mao Zedong

Bulgaria, East Germany, and North Korea. In 1949 China, the world's most populous country, came under communist rule. At this point a great stretch of the world from the Pacific to central Europe was under communist control.

The Cold War

From the late 1940s to the late 1980s, the Soviet Union faced capitalist North America and Western Europe in a confrontation known as the Cold War. The United States, by far the most powerful country in the West, dedicated itself to eradicating communism. It argued that it was protecting the "free world." **Social democrat** parties placed themselves solidly on the American side in the Cold War, confirming their commitment to democracy and individual freedom.

Soviet tanks on the streets of Budapest during the crushing of the Hungarian uprising in October 1956.

French communists demonstrate in Paris in 1947. The Communist Party was a significant force in French politics up to the 1990s.

During the 1950s many people in the West who had previously been communists or sympathized with the Soviet Union sharply altered their views. One reason was Soviet behavior in Eastern Europe. Communist governments were imposed on countries such as Poland, Czechoslovakia, and Hungary and all opposition was brutally suppressed. In 1956, when Hungarians rebelled against communist rule, the Soviet Union sent in tanks to crush the uprising. In the same year, Stalin's successor as Soviet leader, Nikita Khrushchev, publicly admitted to some of the horrors of Stalin's rule. Many former sympathizers reluctantly accepted that Soviet communism was a force for oppression, not liberation.

Yet the threat to capitalism from Soviet-style communism seemed very real. This was not just because of the military power of the Soviet Union. The Soviets had proved that a different way of running a modern economy—through state control, state ownership, and state planning—could be made to work. Communist parties even enjoyed popular support in some Western European democracies, notably France and Italy. Khrushchev once claimed that **socialism** would bury **capitalism.** It did not seem an impossible future.

Developing Nations and the New Left

Today's anticapitalism protests grew directly out of radical movements of the 1950s and 1960s. This was a time of resistance to Western **capitalism** in parts of Africa, Asia, and South America, and of political protest in Europe and North America, especially among young people. The young protesters of the 1960s in particular invented styles of political action that have continued to the present day.

In the second half of the 20th century, it became customary to talk of the globe as divided into three "worlds": the First World of the highly developed Western capitalist countries and Japan; the Second World of the communist countries, stretching from Eastern Europe to the Pacific; and the Third World, made up of the developing nations of Africa, Latin America, and much of Asia. Most people in developing nations lived in extreme poverty, and many developing nations were under colonial rule. Not surprisingly, these countries became an area where revolutionary activity and socialist ideas gathered force. Today some people consider the term Third World offensive.

Multinational companies based in the developed world have been blamed for devastating forests in developing countries. Here a dirt road cuts into the remote rain forest in Borneo to provide access for logging vehicles.

National independence
Between 1947 and the mid-1970s, most colonies became independent, some peacefully and some only after prolonged armed struggles against the **colonial powers**. But it was clear that political independence in itself would not solve the problems of poverty and **underdevelopment**, or put the newly independent countries on an equal footing with their former colonial masters. They were still powerless in the face

of the capitalist system. They had to turn to the former colonial powers for investment and technology, and sell their goods in a world market controlled by big businesses and financiers located in the West. Looking for a way forward, many leaders in developing nations took the Soviet Union or China as their model and adopted socialist economic policies. Almost all believed the pursuit of rapid industrialization was the only path to economic development.

American involvement

From the 1950s onward, the United States became determined to limit the spread of communism. It was actively involved in either supporting or opposing governments in developing nations, depending on whether they seemed to be for or against the capitalist West. Many governments supported by the United States were undemocratic, corrupt, denied their people essential human rights, and used methods such as torture against their opponents. This was especially true in Latin America, where various **left-wing guerrilla** and terrorist groups took on American-backed **military regimes** in the 1960s and 1970s.

In Chile in 1973 the United States even backed a **military coup** to overthrow a democratically elected left-wing government. Americans may have seen this as defending the "free world" against communist oppression, but to many of the world's poorest people the United States simply appeared to be bent on keeping them in poverty so that American business interests (and thereby global capitalism) could flourish.

In 1973 the United States helped Chilean army leader General Pinochet (left) overthrow the democratically elected government of President Salvador Allende (right).

Communism takes root

Two places in which communism was successfully established were the island of Cuba in the Caribbean and Vietnam in Southeast Asia. In Cuba Fidel Castro came to power at the end of the 1950s, after fighting a guerrilla war against a **right-wing** dictatorship. Castro declared his country communist and formed close links with the Soviet Union. The United States imposed a **trade blockade** on Cuba, backed an invasion of the island by Cuban exiles in 1961, and attempted to assassinate Castro, but the communist regime, and its leader, survived.

In the 1960s the United States became heavily involved in the defense of capitalist South Vietnam against a **guerrilla** uprising backed by communist-ruled North Vietnam. Despite a massive commitment of military power—some 50,000 American soldiers died in the conflict—the United States was unable to achieve its objectives. In 1975, two years after the withdrawal of American forces, South Vietnam and its neighbors Cambodia and Laos all came under communist control.

Radical movements in the West

It was not surprising that revolutionary **socialism** and communism should have flourished in the developing countries. But it was startling that the 1960s and 1970s should have brought a wave

The deployment of American soldiers in Vietnam failed to stop the spread of communism in Southeast Asia.

Overthrowing Western society

In 1967 Stokely Carmichael, a Black Power activist in the United States, declared his support for the oppressed of the developing world:

"Our enemy is white Western **imperialist** society.... Our struggle is to overthrow this system which feeds itself and expands itself through the economic and cultural exploitation of nonwhite, non-Western peoples—the Third World."

of radical and revolutionary movements to North America, Western Europe, and Japan. These were areas enjoying prosperity on an unprecedented scale. Rapid economic growth, generally combined with greater equality, meant that most of the population was strikingly better off than ever before. Average industrial workers' wages doubled in Western Europe between 1950 and 1965. Most people not only had new possessions—television sets, family cars, washing machines, refrigerators—but also better food and health care, better education and housing.

This prosperity was provided by **capitalism,** although not unbridled capitalism. For example, governments exercise tight controls on the movement of money across their borders. They also often intervened in the working of the economy to avoid any return to the mass unemployment of the Great Depression. Most countries in Western Europe had what was called a "mixed economy," with some major industries under state control, as in a socialist system, but the overall economy working on free-market capitalist principles.

Ernesto "Che" Guevara

Argentinian-born revolutionary Ernesto "Che" Guevara (1928–1967) was a hero to thousands of radicals in the 1960s. After fighting in the war that brought Fidel Castro to power in Cuba in 1959, Guevara embarked on a personal mission to encourage guerrilla uprisings in other developing countries, among poor peasants whom he regarded as victims of capitalist exploitation. He believed that faced with "many Vietnams," the United States, the leader of the capitalist world, would be overstretched and encircled by revolutionary states. Guevara was killed in Bolivia in 1967, after his small group of guerrillas was ambushed.

Che Guevara (on extreme left of photo) and Fidel Castro (standing) in the mountains of the Sierra Maestra during the guerrilla campaign in Cuba in the 1950s.

Most countries also had some form of welfare with publicly funded health and education services, social security, and state pensions providing support "from the cradle to the grave." Taxation was widely used to redistribute wealth from the rich to the poor, especially in countries where **social democrat** parties were in power all or part of the time—as in Sweden and Britain.

Youth culture

Yet amid this growing prosperity a new wave of anticapitalism and radical protest gathered strength, especially among young people, present in society in especially large numbers because of the post-World War II "baby boom." The youth culture, centered on rock/pop music, challenged Cold War world views and became increasingly antiauthority—against teachers, parents, and other "old" people (a famous saying of the time was "never trust anyone over 30"). The growing prosperity and increasing opportunities brought by an expanding economy tended to make the young scornful of the cautious, narrow views of their elders. The more idealistic young people sensed that they could make a better world than the old men who ruled the world; in 1960 the political leaders of the United States, Germany, France, and Britain were respectively 70, 84, 70, and 66 years old.

There were plenty of causes for protest. Racism was a problem throughout the United States, especially in the South. Many students had their first experience of organized protest as part of the hard-fought campaign for racial equality in the 1950s and 1960s.

> ### Consumer action
> In 1965 Ralph Nader published *Unsafe at Any Speed,* a scathing attack on American car makers for failing to make cars safe to drive. Nader helped start a new form of opposition to **capitalism,** called "consumer activism." It was based on the recognition that people were getting a bad deal from large corporations not as workers, but as consumers of shoddy or dangerous products. Consumer activism has been especially important in campaigns for food safety. In 2000 Ralph Nader ran for President as the Green Party candidate.

Civil rights leader Martin Luther King Jr. (second from left) leads a protest march against unemployment in the 1960s.

Another focus for protest was the threat of nuclear war. The Campaign for Nuclear Disarmament (CND) organized many mass protests, especially in the early 1960s. From the mid-1960s onward, American involvement in the Vietnam War led tens of thousands of people to attend mass protests and carry out acts of **civil disobedience,** convinced that there was no justification for the intervention that was causing military and civilian casualties on a massive scale.

Beatniks and hippies

There was also a wider sense of dissatisfaction with the prosperous "consumer society" that postwar economic growth had created. Young people, inspired by "beatniks" and "hippies," wanted to remove themselves from the drudgery of regular work and the money-ridden, **materialistic** "rat-race" society. During the 1960s experiments in communal living revived the ideals of the early socialists, with hundreds of young people attempting to establish small communities where all property was shared and the products of urban industrial society were shunned. Although not many people went to such extremes, there was a widespread feeling that **capitalism** was delivering the goods but not the good life.

The voice of the New Left

Clear-cut radical political ideas were restricted to a minority, mostly students at the fast-expanding universities. There the ideas of the "New Left" were influential. These were **Marxists** who spoke the language of **class conflict** and "revolutionary socialism." They had no time for Soviet-style communism. Now one of the world's two "superpowers," engaged in a contest with the United States to see who could produce the most powerful rockets and nuclear weapons, the Soviet Union was clearly not attempting to create any kind of ideal socialist society. To the New Left, the Soviet Union was a mirror image of Western capitalist society—different, perhaps, but equally oppressive and

"Using the media

With little mass organization behind them, the 1960s radicals depended on the mass media, especially television, to give their words and actions a large-scale impact. Writing in the underground paper *International Times* in 1967, radical Tom McGrath said that the protesters "have an instinctive understanding of … how to use the media to strongest advantage. In an instant-communication age, any act anywhere can be given worldwide significance if your communication link-up is efficient enough." This lesson has been learned by contemporary anticapitalists, who operate by creating a media spectacle that is a substitute for a mass organization of the kind old-fashioned socialists used to form.

Young people protest against the Vietnam War in the 1960s.

exploitative. Soviet leaders were elderly, white, male, and dull. Youthful idealists looking forward to the revolutionary overthrow of capitalism were forced to search elsewhere for inspiration.

Some of the New Left put their faith in a series of revolutions in developing countries. The **guerrilla** wars that had brought revolution to China, Cuba, and North Vietnam were seen as an example that could be imitated across the developing world. Other New Leftists, including the Trotskyists, continued to have faith in revolution in the heartland of capitalism—Western Europe and North America. Even if Western factory workers would not revolt, the New Left hoped that others would, from students disillusioned with life under capitalism to victims of discrimination and oppression, such as poor African Americans and immigrant workers in Europe.

Subverting capitalism

It was in the 1960s that the environmentally friendly bicycle became a symbol of opposition to the polluting, car-driving capitalist world. In 1965 the Dutch **anarchist** Provo (short for Provocation) group published a **manifesto** stating that "we live in a ... sick society," in which we are told "what we should do, what we should consume...." As an act of subversion against this "sick society," the Provos left thousands of white bicycles on the streets of Amsterdam. These were free for anyone to ride. People borrowing the bicycles were expected to leave them when they had finished their journey for someone else to use. This was supposed to stop people from using cars—or in the Provos' words, end the "terror of the motorized **bourgeoisie**."

Protesting Capitalism

Until the second half of the 1960s, most people regarded the New Left talk of a possible "revolution" in Western societies as evidence of how laughably out of touch "hippies" were with reality. But, as the number and scale of protests in different Western countries mounted, the possibility of revolutionary upheaval began to be more likely. This was especially true among students. By 1970, it was claimed, more than a million American students were prepared to describe themselves as "revolutionaries."

May 1968

In May 1968 clashes between students and police in Paris, France sparked a general strike by workers that paralyzed the country for a month. In the same year, students and workers in former Czechoslovakia rebelled against communist rule. Students mounted a spectacular challenge to authority in Italy and West Germany, and confronted police on university campuses across the United States. In August, a confrontation between anti-Vietnam War protesters and police turned the center of Chicago into a battleground during the National Democratic Convention.

May 1968: in Paris, police clashed with rioting students, many of whom wished for a new form of society to replace industrial capitalism.

The dominant mood of the 1968 revolts was of idealistic anarchism. One German student leader, Rudi Deutschke, said that the aim was "an end to the power of people over people." Most of the student radicals did not want to replace existing governments with a new government; they wanted no government at all. The 1968 radicals relied on direct action—especially confrontation with the

Developing Nations and the New Left

A young protester confronts a Soviet tank after the Soviet invasion of Czechoslovakia in 1968.

police—and catchy slogans. The style of protest had an element of zaniness and fun that was quite different from the earnestness of traditional Marxism and **socialism.** In the United States, for example, the Yippies (Youth International Party), led by Abbie Hoffman, proposed putting forward a pig as a candidate in the elections for U.S. president.

Asking for everything
Characteristic of the student revolts of the 1960s was a refusal to accept what are generally considered to be the normal realities of everyday life—the need to work, earn money, be less than happy much of the time. One famous 1960s slogan was: *"Be realistic—demand the impossible."* Another, shouted during demonstrations, was: *"What do we want? Everything! When do we want it? Now!"*

In truth there was little realistic chance that the student radicals, **Marxists,** and **anarchists** could seriously overthrow the order of society. Soviet tanks crushed the student and worker rebellion in Czechoslovakia, while in France and the United States democratic elections in 1968 brought resounding victories for those candidates most outspokenly opposed to the student revolts. In additon, many radical groups succumbed to external suppression and internal conflicts.

Campaigns of terror

After their defeat in 1968, some radicals who remained committed to the violent overthrow of the capitalist system turned to terrorism. These post-1968 terrorist groups included the Red Brigades in Italy, the Baader-Meinhof Red Army Faction in West Germany, and the Weathermen (also known as the Weather Underground) in the United States.

Through the 1970s such groups carried out bombings, kidnappings, and assassinations. In Italy, for example, the Red Brigades kidnapped and murdered the prime minister, Aldo Moro, in 1978. The West German Baader-Meinhof group formed an alliance with Palestinian terrorists in the Middle East, carrying out some spectacular terrorist actions, including hijackings of airliners. The immediate terrorist wave had subsided by the end of the 1970s, but international terrorism was to be one of the most lasting contributions this period made to history.

Tradition of protest

Far more of the 1968 radicals found more peaceful directions for their energies. In the 1970s protest movements continued to flourish, but mostly with more-specific, less wide-ranging aims. The Women's Movement became a major force, launching an immensely effective assault on male authority and

Taking a new path

Green Party activist Jonathan Porritt explained that ecology parties were opposed to all existing political movements, whether procapitalist, communist, or **social democrat,** because these were all obsessed with maximizing industrial production:

"The politics of the Industrial Age, left, right, and center, is like a three-lane motorway [highway], with different vehicles in different lanes, but all heading in the same direction. Greens feel that it is the very direction that is wrong ... the motorway of industrialization inevitably leads to the abyss—hence our decision to get off it, and seek an entirely different direction."

privilege. Homosexuals campaigned for equal rights in the Gay Liberation movement. The fight against racism continued to concern many.

The ecology movement also took off. The international environmental campaigning organization Greenpeace was founded in 1971, for example, and Green parties were founded that went on to win considerable electoral support, most notably in West Germany. The ecology movement challenged both the capitalist and communist worlds, with their polluting industries and obsession with economic growth. The main challenge now was to regulate industrial production in order to protect the world from further environmental destruction. The 1960s radicals had failed to bring about a revolution, but they had established a new tradition of protest that would not fade away.

This 1983 election poster for the German Green Party says, "We have only borrowed the Earth from our children."

Opposing Global Capitalism

The 1980s were a decade of triumph for global **capitalism** and disaster for communism. This was a sudden and unexpected reversal. During the 1970s the capitalist world still seemed on the defensive. Countries adopting, or taken over by, communist or communist-backed regimes in that decade included South Vietnam, Cambodia, Laos, Angola, Mozambique, Ethiopia, Nicaragua, and Afghanistan. But the United States fought back by turning **guerrilla** war, traditionally a method employed by **left-wing** revolutionaries, against these left-wing regimes. U.S.-backed guerrillas fought against the communist regimes in Nicaragua, Angola, Mozambique, and Afghanistan. The Soviet army became engaged in a war against anti-communist guerrillas in Afghanistan that much resembled America's disastrous war in Vietnam.

Falling behind

It was increasingly evident that the communist's state-controlled **economic system**, the only existing alternative to capitalism, was not working. In the state-controlled economies of the Soviet Union and Eastern Europe, output and living standards were falling further and further behind the capitalist West. Industry in communist countries was less efficient, and more technologically backward and polluting than that

The stock market

Communism wasn't the only system to suffer a failure in the 1980s. In October of 1987 the **stock market** suffered its biggest crash since the Great Depression (see p. 27). It suffered another crash in 1989. The stock market is a complex system that allows companies to raise money by selling parts of itself in the form of "stocks." The stock market is the name of the industry in which stocks and bonds (the government equivalent of stocks) are sold. Once a share of stock is bought, it becomes the property of the buyer who can sell it to whomever he or she wishes. People buy stocks because they hope the stocks will increase in value and can then be sold at a profit. Although many people make their living by forecasting which stocks will rise in value, there is no way of knowing for sure. Recent stock market failures and crashes have shown that investing in the market is a form of gambling.

in the West. Although most people in the communist-ruled countries had secure employment and an adequate pension in old age, this security was at the expense of a lack of basic human rights and shortages of most consumer goods.

The collapse of communism

In the early 1980s, the Solidarity union staged strikes and mass protests in communist-ruled Poland, demanding both political rights and better living conditions. Although no one knew it at the time, this was the first step toward the collapse of Soviet communism. In 1985 a dynamic, relatively young communist, Mikhail Gorbachev, became leader of the Soviet Union and introduced major reforms in an attempt to reverse economic decline. As these reforms swept through the Soviet Union and Eastern Europe, popular protest mounted and communist rulers lost their grip on power.

In 1989 Germany's Berlin Wall—which had been built by the Soviet Union in 1961 to separate communist-ruled East Berlin from capitalist-controlled West Berlin—was broken down. Only two years later, the Soviet Communist Party was banned and the Soviet Union itself fell apart. China stayed under the control of the Communist Party, but its rulers largely abandoned communist economic policies, instead adopting **free-market** capitalism in an attempt to create economic growth.

For many the tearing down of the Berlin Wall in 1989 symbolized the failure of the communist political and economic system. It opened the way for the introduction of capitalism throughout the former Soviet countries.

Privatization

Communism had suddenly ceased to exist as a rival to **capitalism.** Meanwhile social democracy in the West was also under attack. In Britain, for example, Margaret Thatcher, Conservative prime minister between 1979 and 1990, set out to reverse much of what the Labour movement had achieved over the years, cutting back on social security, pensions, and state-funded health care. She also returned state-owned industries to private ownership, in a process known as "privatization," and curbed the power of the **labor unions.** To differing degrees similar changes took place in most Western countries. At the same time, the kind of industries whose workers had provided the backbone of support for **socialism**—coal mining, shipbuilding, iron, and steel—were in sharp decline. **Social democrat** parties were obliged to water down the socialist element of their policies further and further to maintain support from voters.

Margaret Thatcher, British prime minister from 1979 to 1990, believed in a return to unbridled free-market capitalism. Her tough line with those who disagreed, especially labor unionists, earned her the nickname the "Iron Lady."

Globalization

As Soviet communism collapsed and democratic socialism waned, capitalism was entering an aggressive new phase. Businesses operating under the capitalist system continued to grow, merging or swallowing up smaller enterprises to create giant corporations. In their pursuit of higher profits and broader markets, capitalist businesses pushed further than before in the process known as **globalization**.

Globalization essentially means the whole world becoming a single economic unit, in which a small number of huge multinational companies would play a dominant role. It was at root a natural product of technological progress, which was making the world seem like a smaller place. From the 1970s onward, the increasing use of computers and satellite communications made the movement of money and information from continent to continent almost instantaneous, while the growth of air travel allowed goods and people to move around the world far more quickly and easily than ever before. But this technological advance was accompanied by a deliberate political decision to return capitalism more or less to the classic form it had taken before 1914. Tarrifs, trade agreements, and other barriers to the movement of capital around the world were systematically removed. This return to classic capitalism is known as "neoliberalism." It showed a revival of the belief that if only governments would get out of the way and allow capitalists to trade and invest freely, prosperity would result.

Controlling global capitalism

One of the most unlikely critics of globalization to emerge in the 1990s was George Soros, a prominent financier who had made billions speculating on world financial markets. Soros argued that the global capitalist system needed to be brought under political control. He wrote:

"I do not want to abolish capitalism. In spite of its shortcomings, it is better than the alternatives.... [But] to stabilize and regulate a truly global economy, we need some global system of political decision-making. In short we need a global society to support our global economy."

The power of the multinationals

The lifting of barriers on the movement of money and goods meant that multinational companies were independent of—in some ways far more powerful than—national governments. They could invest their cash and locate their factories or offices anywhere in the world—wherever labor was cheap and loosely regulated and governments were favorably disposed toward foreign businesses making profits. If workers asked for better wages and conditions or governments pursued even vaguely "socialist" policies, the multinationals could take their investment and factories elsewhere.

The new global **capitalism** and "neoliberalism" were imposed on the governments and people of the developing world by pressure from international organizations. The International Monetary Fund (IMF) is an organization set up to support countries in economic difficulties and maintain financial stability across the world. Yet it only lends money to countries that agree to cut government spending by reducing social programs to manageable levels. The General Agreement on Tariff and Trade (GATT) and its 1995 successor, the World Trade Organization (WTO), pressed countries into removing barriers to the import of goods from abroad and abandoning all measures to support or subsidize their own locally based businesses.

To many people in smaller countries it seemed that the WTO was working to benefit the multinationals and prevent countries from developing their economies. For example, some banana growers on Caribbean islands, organized into cooperatives, were producing bananas that they exported to Europe on a small scale. The European Union imported these bananas on favorable terms, as a way of encouraging

Opposing Global Capitalism

the Caribbean banana growers who were struggling to escape from poverty. But the WTO took the view that the European Union had to give equal treatment to bananas from large banana plantations run by American companies in countries such as Guatemala. If the European Union followed the WTO line, then the Caribbean growers faced ruin, as they would not be able to compete with the American companies, which could produce bananas more cheaply.

Antiglobalization

Supporters of **globalization** and neo-liberalism argued that globalization would lead to rapid economic growth across the world and offered all countries the best prospect of prosperity. But critics saw it as giving a free hand to multinationals to **exploit** the poorest of the Earth's people and destroy the natural environment. Throughout the 1990s antiglobalization became a fresh focus for protest movements.

A McDonald's fast-food outlet in Karachi, Pakistan is a striking example of the penetration of Western-based multinational businesses into every part of the world.

Modern radical protest, established in the 1960s, had continued through the decades, with ecological concerns increasingly holding center stage. Protesters gathered wherever a new nuclear power plant, highway or airport was being built, mobilizing public opinion against damage to the environment and threats to public health. Animal rights activists called for an end to factory-farming methods, and attacked the fur trade and the laboratory testing of cosmetics on animals.

Multinational burgers

A good example of the extraordinary expansion of multinational businesses over the last two decades is the growth of the McDonald's fast-food restaurant chain. By the early 21st century, there were McDonald's outlets in 120 countries. At one time new branches were opening at the rate of four a day. It was estimated that, every day, one in 200 of the world's entire population ate at McDonald's.

Protesting Capitalism

Activists within the Women's Movement not only fought for equal rights for their sex, but also called for an end to the aggressive and destructive relationship to the Earth. This, they argued, was typical of societies controlled by men, societies that were technology oriented and bent on the "conquest of nature." More traditional socialist and **anarchist** concerns about poverty and inequality, and the domination of the world by the power of money, had also continued to gain support.

Environmentalists

Free-market globalization touched on all of these concerns. Environmentalists argued that the activities of multinationals had to be controlled if they were to be prevented from exhausting the earth's nonrenewable resources, destroying rain forests, polluting land and sea, and increasing global warming. Behind every new perceived threat to the environment—for example, from **genetically modified (GM) crops**, which became an issue

Forests not for sale

Forest-dwellers in India have protested attempts, supported by international organizations, to make commercial use of the forests. They stated:

"For the World Bank and the World Trade Organization, our forests are a marketable commodity. But for us, the forests are a home, our source of livelihood, the dwelling of our gods, the burial ground of our ancestors, the inspiration of our culture.... We will not let you sell our forests. So go back from our forests and our country."

Greenpeace activists attack an experimental planting of GM corn in eastern England in 1999. Protesters saw GM crops as an example of big business threatening the environment for profit.

in the late 1990s—there seemed to be a multinational company trying to increase its profits. At the same time, the question of inequality continued to plague **capitalism** as it had from the earliest days. Capitalism could create even more wealth, and raise the general standard of living for business owners, governments, and the middle classes, but at the same time created extreme poverty for the poorest people. Welfare spending cuts and other measures imposed by the IMF were a direct attack on the living standards of some of the world's poorest people. And, in the 1990s, poor countries were actually paying more to the richest countries in debt repayments than they were receiving in aid.

Issues such as world poverty and environmental damage were acknowledged as subjects for discussion by governments, by well-established pressure groups such as Greenpeace and by the **United Nations**, through bodies such as the UN Commission on Sustainable Development. But anticapitalism radicals felt more direct action was needed. A wave of antiglobalization protests grew during the 1990s. These antiglobalization protests included the work of new, smaller, and decentralized groups, as well as larger, more well-established, nationally organized groups, including Greenpeace, the AFL-CIO **labor union,** and factions within various Protestant and Catholic curches.

The Ogoni oilfields

Protesters in the developing world sometimes faced harassment and worse from the authorities. In Nigeria, for example, the minority Ogoni people of the Niger delta claimed that multinational oil companies exploiting oil reserves on their territory had created an ecological disaster. In return for seeing the fish and shellfish they used to eat poisoned by oil slicks, and their land crisscrossed with massive pipelines, the Ogoni argued they had received nothing, neither jobs nor the investment to provide basic services such as electricity or clean drinking water. But when the Ogoni organized a protest movement, the Nigerian authorities reacted with great severity. In 1995 nine leaders of the movement, including writer Ken Saro-Wiwa, were found guilty on trumped-up charges and executed by hanging.

The protesters

In Europe and North America, the protesters were a mix of **Marxist** revolutionary socialists, radical labor unionists, women's groups, environmental activists, **anarchists,** and animal rights groups. In the developing world, resistance to global **capitalism** came mostly from the rural population, who saw their way of life and living standards threatened by the new wave of capitalist economic development. Prominent among groups confronting capitalism in developing countries were the Zapatistas, representing Indian peasants in Mexico, the Landless movement representing the poorest people of Brazil, and various farmers' organizations in India, especially the Narmada Bachao Andolan (NBA), formed to resist the building of the Narmada dam.

Carnival against capital

Making extensive use of the Internet as a method of organization starting in the mid-1990s, networks were formed among the groups in both the industrialized countries and in the developing world. This led to coordinated actions such as international days of protest. On June 18, 1999, for example, a "carnival against capital" was held in cities around the world, including London and New York. The focus of protest became the increasingly frequent meetings of world leaders and multinational trade regulators, which were considered essential precisely because of the need to deal with issues raised by the global economy. Protesters made their presence felt from the Seattle meeting of the WTO in 1999 (see page 4) to

Globalized protest

The anticapitalism movement was itself partly a product of globalization as the world began to seem smaller because of improved communication and transportation. The Internet made possible the direct link-up between small groups in many parts of the world without any cumbersome organization involving leaders and membership cards. International protesters were also able to assemble swiftly at any point in the world to stage a demonstration. For example, anticapitalists from Mexico, Bangladesh, or Thailand would take part in protests in the Czech Republic, Spain, or Canada. This was sometimes described as "globalization from the bottom up," as opposed to capitalism's "globalization from the top down."

The "carnival against capital" held in cities around the world, including London, June 1999.

the American Free Trade Area Summit in Quebec in April 2001, the European Union Summit in Barcelona in March 2002, and the Earth Summit in South Africa in August 2002.

These anticapitalism activists differed in some ways from the disciplined ranks and mass movements of earlier **socialism.** However, they were extremely influential, since the protesters were only one wing of a movement of criticism of **globalization** that also included such respectable bodies as United Nations commissions, major **nongovernmental organizations**, and many governments of countries in the developing world.

Anticapitalism principles

Peoples' Global Action (PGA), one of the most prominent groupings in the anticapitalism movement, describes itself as a network coordinating the struggle of "all those who fight the destruction of humanity and the planet by capitalism." The declared principles of the PGA are typical of the anticapitalism movement. They include: "a very clear rejection of capitalism, imperialism, and **feudalism**, all trade agreements, institutions, and governments that promote destructive globalization;" the rejection of "all forms of domination and discrimination including ... **patriarchy**, racism, and religious fundamentalism ..." and a belief in "a confrontational attitude ... direct action and civil disobedience."

Into the 21st Century

By the beginning of the 21st century New York, the largest city in the United States, the home of the **United Nations**, the World Trade Center, and many multinational corporations, was widely seen as the hub of global **capitalism**. On September 11, 2001, **Islamic fundamentalist** terrorists destroyed the World Trade Center, killing thousands of innocent people.

The vast majority of Muslims and members of Western anticapitalism movements did not support the September 11 attack. They rejected both Islamic fundamentalism and terrorism. But many nonetheless regarded it as the expression of a justified anger, an understandable reaction to the injustice that condemned much of the world's population to powerlessness and extreme poverty.

Defenders of capitalism

Procapitalists argue that this attitude is irrational. They take a positive view of capitalism's past and future impact on the world. They point out that it has brought great prosperity to a considerable part of the world's population, notably in Europe and North America, and say that over time it will do the same for the rest of the world. After all, some developing countries that have encouraged

September 11, 2001: terrorists destroy New York's World Trade Center, symbolic hub of global capitalism.

Learn to love wealth

In 1998, in his book *Eat the Rich*, the American **right-wing** journalist P. J. O'Rourke vigorously expresses the procapitalist position. He argues that the quickest way to reduce poverty in the developing world is to let capitalists make as much money as possible, without worrying about equality:

"If we want the whole world to be rich, we need to start loving wealth. In the difference between poverty and plenty, the problem is the poverty, not the difference."

No more hunger

Speaking in 2000, Eric Hobsbawm, a distinguished historian highly critical of capitalism, argued nonetheless that living standards of the world's population have improved because of the global economy:

"We have today three times the [world] population there was at the start of the 20th century, and all these people are physically stronger, taller, longer living, and healthier. They suffer less hunger and famine, enjoy a higher income, and have an immeasurably greater access to goods and services.... This is also true of poorer countries.... Hunger in most of the world ... is no longer something that human beings are obliged to live with."

private enterprise, for example, South Korea and Taiwan, have achieved a spectacular rise in living standards in a few decades.

Many procapitalists do not reject the concerns raised by the anticapitalism movement. They accept, to a greater or lesser degree, the need to limit damage to the environment or to help eradicate world poverty. But they believe that these goals can be achieved either by mildly reforming the way capitalism works through government intervention and regulation, or even by *more* capitalism—for example, by making environmentally friendly projects profitable for business corporations to carry out.

Taiwanese workers assemble motherboards for computers. Countries such as Taiwan and South Korea have been successful modern examples of capitalist enterprise, experiencing a dramatic rise in living standards.

The anticapitalism arguments

Anticapitalists argue that **free-market capitalism** must inevitably impoverish many to profit a few. They point to the environmental damage being caused by multinational corporations either unable or unwilling to do anything to control it. They point to the undemocratic nature of the global system, in which even where elected governments exist, they are largely powerless in the face of global capitalism. They see poverty increasing, not decreasing, as **globalization** spreads—witness the mass of **economic migrants** trying to enter the world's richer states from the poorer ones. Russia is a good example of the possible negative effects of capitalism, the change from communism to free-market capitalism in the 1990s has led to a sharp rise in poverty and a sharp fall in life expectancy.

Traditional rights

In some ways the anticapitalism movement can be seen as conservative, rather than revolutionary. Most of the protests are an attempt to resist change and defend traditional rights. These rights may be the way of life of forest dwellers and peasant farmers in the developing world or, in the developed world, the hard-won rights of **labor unionists,** the welfare state, or unspoiled rural areas threatened by road-building.

However, anticapitalism is also inspired by a vision of the future that has much, though not everything, in common with the old socialist tradition. It is a vision

All life is precious

In 1999 the League of Revolutionaries for a New America expressed the view that capitalism was the obstacle blocking the way to a better world:

"For the first time in history, technological innovations have given society the means to produce an absolute abundance.... The new wealth generated by these changes is not being shared by all. Instead, obscene riches are being accumulated at one pole of society, while a more and more brutal poverty is created at the other.... Our society can either move to a police state that upholds repression and enforces suffering, or it can move forward to a new stage of human development that cherishes and nurtures the lives of all."

Into the 21st Century

> ## Changing history
> Speaking in the 1990s of the many different movements opposing capitalism, from peasant groups in Mexico and Brazil to antiglobalization protesters in the industrialized countries, American radical Noam Chomsky said:
>
> *"If these diverse, dispersed movements everywhere manage to create bonds of solidarity and support ... together they will be able to change the course of contemporary history."*

of humans living in harmony with their environment and with one another, respecting animals as well as their fellow human beings, tending planet Earth to create a sustainable future. Economic growth would still take place, but in a form that is not destructive of the earth's resources and that is beneficial to all people, not just a few. And people in local communities would have power over their own lives, building links with other communities across the world.

The fall of global capitalism, so often predicted over the last two centuries, looks as unlikely at the start of the third millennium as it ever did. The anticapitalism movement might help set the agenda on world poverty or environmental issues, but it does not imagine it will "seize power" by overthrowing national governments. Any form of world revolution is a distant concept. Yet the vision of a better, even ideal, world of equal sharing, peace, mutual respect, and harmony continues to exist as a driving force in contemporary anticapitalist movements.

Confrontations between riot police and anticapitalist protesters are frequent in the first decade of the 21st century.

Protesting Capitalism

Timeline

1811 — "Luddites," poor hand-weavers in England opposed to the introduction of weaving machinery, attack factories and destroy machines

1813 — Robert Owen publishes *A New View of Society*, one of the earliest statements of socialist views

1834 — The Tolpuddle Martyrs are found guilty of forming a trade union and deported to Australia

1839 — Britain launches the first Opium War against China to force the Chinese to open their ports to foreign trade

1844 — Britain's first cooperative store is set up in Rochdale, Lancashire

1848 — The *Communist Manifesto*, written by Karl Marx and his associate Friedrich Engels, calls for a workers' revolution to overthrow capitalism

1864 — The International Working Men's Association, or First International, is founded to coordinate the actions of socialists and revolutionaries in different countries

1867 — Karl Marx publishes the first volume of *Das Kapital* (Capital), his immensely influential analysis of, and attack on, capitalism

1871 — A popular uprising in Paris creates the Paris Commune, a revolutionary government that is soon crushed with great loss of life

1889 — The Second International is founded, an international organization that is joined by most socialist parties

1903 — A split in the Russian Social Democratic Party leaves V. I. Lenin as head of the Bolshevik faction

1905 — International Workers of the World, an anarchist union movement dedicated to class warfare, is founded in the United States

1906 — The British Labour Party, originally founded in 1900 as the Labour Representation Committee, has 26 members elected to Parliament

1914 — Start of World War I

1917 — The Bolshevik seizure of power in the Russian Revolution establishes the world's first long-lived anticapitalism government, leading to the formation of the Soviet Union in 1923

1918 — World War I ends

1924 — The first Labour government comes to power in Britain; it lasts less than a year

1929 — A stock-market crash marks the beginning of the Great Depression

1929 — Dictator Josef Stalin initiates rapid industrialization and state control of agriculture in the Soviet Union

1933 — U.S. President F. D. Roosevelt initiates the New Deal, abandoning many of the principles of free-market capitalism in response to the Depression and mass unemployment

1939 — Start of World War II

1945 — Victory against Nazi Germany leaves the Soviet Union in control of Central Europe, World War II ends

1945 — A Labour government is elected in Britain by a large majority; it takes the major industries into public ownership and founds a welfare state

1949	Communists led by Mao Zedong take power in China; an alternative system to capitalism prevails from the Pacific Ocean to Central Europe
1959	Guerrilla leader Fidel Castro takes power in Cuba, soon declaring his allegiance to communism
1968	Riots and protests, in which left-wing students play a leading part, sweep Western Europe and North America
1971	The environmental campaigning organization Greenpeace is founded
1978	The Italian prime minister, Aldo Moro, is kidnapped and murdered by members of the Red Brigades
1980	Deng Xiao-ping leads China towards capitalist-style free-market economic policies, although the Communist Party remains in power
1985	Mikhail Gorbachev becomes head of the Soviet Union and tries to reform its economic and political system
1989	The fall of the Berlin Wall marks the collapse of Communist government across Central Europe
1991	The Soviet Union ceases to exist
1995	The World Trade Organization (WTO) is founded
1999	Anticapitalist riots rock Seattle during a WTO summit meeting
July 2001	An anticapitalist protester is killed during clashes with police at an economic summit of world leaders in Genoa, Italy
Sept. 2001	Terrorists crash hijacked airliners into the World Trade Center in New York and the Pentagon
March 2002	Mass demonstrations take place during a European summit meeting in Barcelona, Spain
Nov 2002	A huge anticapitalism march takes place peacefully in Florence, Italy

Further Reading

Bookbinder, Steve, and Lynn Einleger. *The Dictionary of the Global Economy*. Danbury, Conn.: Scholastic Library, 2001.

Bowden, Rob. *World Poverty*. Chicago: Raintree, 2003.

Downing, David. *Capitalism*. Chicago: Heinemann, 2002.

Garlake, Teresa. *Global Debt*. Chicago: Raintree, 2003.

Grant, R.G. *Ideas of the Modern World: Capitalism*. Chicago: Raintree, 2001.

Pendergast, Sara, and Tom Pendergast (editors). *Worldbook Encyclopedia of National Economies*. Farmington Hills, Mich.: Gale Group, 2002.

Glossary

anarchist
person who rejects all forms of government and authority

anarcho-syndicalist
member of a movement that wanted to use labor unions as a basis for the violent overthrow of capitalism

bourgeoisie
in the Marxist view of capitalist society, the bourgeoisie is the social class that owns the means of production—factories, machines, etc.—and financial capital. Today the word is also used to refer to members of the middle class, especially those who are happy with a materialistic lifestyle.

bureaucrat
official who runs government departments and state organizations

capitalism
economic system based on private ownership of business and trade

civil disobedience
form of nonviolent protest involving the refusal to obey—or the deliberate breaking of—laws that are regarded as unjust

class conflict
conflict between different groups in society, especially between workers and business owners

collective
large farm run by the state, created by taking over the land of independent peasant farmers

colonial power
state that runs other countries as part of an empire

commune
group of people living together and sharing property and responsibility for work on an equal basis

democracy
political system in which government is run by representatives elected by the people

dictatorial
exercising absolute power

economic migrant
worker who moves around the country or around the world in search of work and a better standard of living

economic system
way the production and distribution of goods and services is organized

egalitarian
promoting the belief that all humans should be equal in respect to social, political, and econonomic privileges

exploit
to abuse someone by paying him or her unfairly or forcing the person to work in unfair conditions. A resource or place is exploited if it is used unfairly.

extremist
someone opposed to compromise or half-measures.

feudalism
economic and social system dominated by an aristocracy of landowners to whom their subjects owe dues and service

free market
international trade that is free of government-imposed restrictions

globalization
breaking down of all barriers to the movement of money or goods between countries, in theory turning the whole world into a single economic unit

genetically modified (GM) crops
crops that have had their genetic material altered by scientists to give them new characteristics

guerrilla
soldier who fights in small-scale hit-and-run warfare; not a member of a regular army

hierarchical
organization of people or things arranged by rank, grade, or class, with those at the top having more power and rights than those at the bottom

Glossary

ideology
set of ideas that expresses the beliefs of a political movement or a government

imperialist person who extends the power or influence of one nation over others, as in an empire

Islamic fundamentalism
movement in Muslim countries that advocates a return to the original principles of the Islamic faith, rejecting any compromise with the modern world or Western capitalism

labor union
organization formed by a group of working people to represent their interests in negotiations or conflict with their employers

left-wing
term used for radical, liberal, socialist, communist, or anarchist political groups or ideas

manifesto
statement of a political program

Marxist
person or government taking some version of the thoughts of Karl Marx as the basis for their political ideas or political system

mass movement
political movement involving many people

materialistic
excessively devoted to making money or accumulating possessions

means of production
tools and raw materials used to create products

militant
very active and uncompromising political activist or movement

military coup
seizure of power by the armed forces

military regime
government run by officers of the armed forces

nongovernmental organization (NGO)
organization that is independent of control by any government

patriarchy
system in which men dominate society and women occupy an inferior position

political activist
someone actively involved in campaigning, protests, and other political action

proletariat
Marxist term for the industrial working class: factory workers, miners, etc.

propaganda
information designed to advance a cause or serve the interests of a government

right-wing
term used for political groups or ideas opposed to communism, socialism, radicalism, or anarchism

shareholder
person who owns shares in a company, usually having bought them on the stock market

social democrat
person who believes, at least to some degree, in socialism, but not at the expense of democracy or individual freedom

socialism
an alternative economic and social system to capitalism, in which extremes of wealth and poverty are eradicated and the economy is run for the good of the community rather than for individual profit

stock market
place where shares in companies are bought and sold

surplus value
product of a worker's labor above and beyond what is required by the worker to live

trade blockade
preventing goods from being imported into or exported out of a country

underdevelopment
term used to describe the situation of countries whose people are poorer than those of the world's richest states, with less productive economies and inferior health care, education, and transport services

United Nations
international body, formed in 1945, with almost all the world's countries as members. It sets international standards, aims to resolve conflicts, and manages relief and development programs.

Index

Numbers in **bold** refer to pages with illustrations.

anarchists 21, 22, 23
anarcho-syndicalists 21, 22

Campaign for Nuclear Disarmament (CND) 39
capitalism 4, 6–7, 8, 10–11, 14, 16, 19, 20, 21, 23, 24, 26, 27, 29, 34, 37, 46, 49, 50, 53, 54, 56–59
carnival against capital 54–**55**,
Castro, Fidel 36, **37**
child labor **9**, 10
civil disobedience 30, 39, 53
class conflict 18, 40
Clinton, President Bill 4
Cold War, the **32**–33
collectivization **29**–30
colonialism 31, 34–35
communes 17
communism 19, 24, 26–**33**, 35, 36, 46–47
cooperatives 17, 50
Czolgosz, Leon **22**, 23

demonstrations 4–5, **7**, 54, **55**, 59
direct action 5, 21, 22, 42

employment reforms 11
Engels, Friedrich **18**, 19
environmentalists **52**, 53,59
European Union 50–51

fascism **28**
Fourier, Charles 17
free market 6, 8

Gandhi, Mohandas 30
Gay Liberation 45
General Agreement on Tariff and Trade (GATT) 50
globalization 4, 7, 49–51, 58

Goldman, Emma **23**
Gorbachev, Mikhail 47
Great Depression, the **27**–28
Green parties 45
Guevara, Ernesto 'Che' **37**
guilds 10

Hitler, Adolf **28**

imperialism 13–14, 36
industrial capitalism 8–9, 12, 14, 24, 42
Industrial Revolution **8–9**, 12, **13**
Industrial Workers of the World (IMW) 22
International Monetary Fund (IMF) 50

Khrushchev, Nikita 33

labor unions 11, 20, **21**, 22, 28, 47, 48, 53, 54
Lenin, Vladimir Ilyich 24, 25, 29
Luddites 8, **10**–11

Mao Zedong **31**
Marx, Karl **18**–19, 20
May Day 23
McKinley, President William **22**, 23
multinational businesses 5, 7, **34**, 49–**51**, 53, 56, 58
Mussolini, Benito 28

Opium Wars 12, **13**
Owen, Robert **16**, 17

privatization 48

revolutions 20, **25**–27, 42
Roosevelt, President Franklin D. 28
Second International 23

slaves 14
social democrats 24, 26, 38, 48
socialism 7, 14, 15, 18, 19, 23, 24, 28, 43, 48
socialists 16–17, 20–21, 22, 25
Solidarity 47
Soviet Union 29–31, 33, 40 46–47
Stalin, Josef 29, 30, 33

terrorism 21, 22, 35, 44
Thatcher, Margaret **48**
Third International 26
Tolpuddle Martyrs 11
Trotsky, Leon 29

United Nations (UN) 53, 55
utopian socialists **16**–17

Vietnam War 36, 39, **41**, 42
voting rights **15**

Women's Movement 44, 52
working conditions **9**–10, 11, 14, 21, 50
World Trade Center **56**
World Trade Organization (WTO) 4–5, 50, 51, 54
World War I 22, 23, 24–25, 27
World War II 31, 38

Yippies 43
youth culture 38, 40–44, **41**, **42, 43**

Lizards

Written by Jo Windsor

In this book you will see lizards.

Some lizards can live in trees.

Some lizards can live on the ground.

Some lizards can go in the water.

Lizards can live...

in trees — Yes? No?

in shoes — Yes? No?

in water — Yes? No?

This lizard lives in a tree.

Look at its toes.

Its toes help the lizard climb.

Its toes help the lizard go up the tree.

toe

This lizard lives on the ground.

It has claws.

Its claws help it to hold on to the rock.

claws

Look at this lizard's feet!

This lizard can run over the sand.

This lizard can run on the water!

This lizard runs on water to...

get food　　　　Yes? No?

swim　　　　　Yes? No?

get away　　　Yes? No?

Look at this lizard's toes!

Its toes help it hold on to the tree.

Look at the lizard's tail!

The lizard's tail helps it hold on to the tree, too.

tail

This lizard can fly!

It lives up in the trees.

It can go from tree to tree.

What can fly?

bird   spider

fly   lizard

crab   duck

Look at all the spikes.

This lizard has lots and lots of spikes.

The spikes are very sharp.

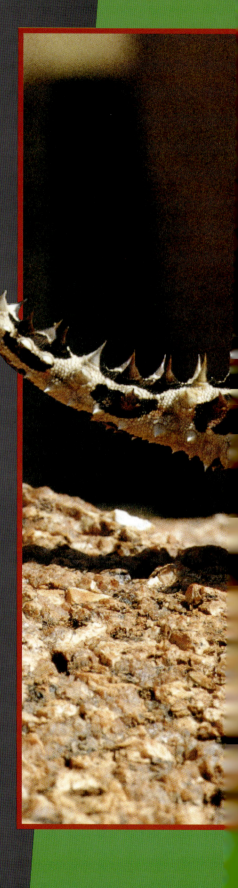

Look at this mouth!

This lizard has a big mouth.

This lizard says, **"Go away!"**

This lizard can look big.

This lizard says, "**Go away!**" too.

A lizard can look big to say "Go away"...

to a bird Yes? No?

to a snake Yes? No?

Look at this lizard.

Look at its mouth!

Index

what lizards have
- claws 3, 8
- feet 3, 10
- mouth 18, 20
- spikes 3, 16
- tail 12
- toes 3, 6, 12

where lizards live
- ground 4, 8
- trees 4, 6, 12, 14
- water 5, 11

A yes/no chart

Lizards can climb trees. **Yes? No?**

Lizards can talk. **Yes? No?**

Lizards can go in the water. **Yes? No?**

Lizards have hats. Yes? No?

Lizards have claws. Yes? No?

Lizards have spikes. Yes? No?

Lizards can eat pizza. Yes? No?

Word Bank

claws

feet

ground

mouth

rocks

sand

spikes

toes

trees

water